"I'll always be with you. Even when you can't see me, I'm with you, watching you from Heaven. You can talk to me, and I'll hear you. And if you let yourself be very still and quiet, and listen not just with your ears, but with your heart, you'll be able to hear me, too."

For Cornelius Patrick McMahon, my Papa. Thank you for the flower.
Love,
Jessica

For Jennifer.
Steve

Library of Congress Cataloging-in-Publication Data
Curtis, Jessica Lynn.
  Papa's new home / written by Jessica Lynn Curtis ; illustrated by Steve Harmon.
      p. cm.
  Summary: After her beloved grandfather dies, Jessie is very sad until Papa, now "shiny and twinkly," visits her one night
to explain about death and give her a glimpse of Heaven.
  ISBN 978-0-931674-64-8 (alk. paper)
  [1. Heaven--Fiction. 2. Grandfathers--Fiction. 3. Death--Fiction. 4. Soul--Fiction.] I. Harmon, Steve, ill. II. Title.
  PZ7.C94183Pap 2012
  [E]--dc23   2011035058

Text copyright © 2012, Jessica Lynn Curtis
Illustrations copyright © 2012, TRISTAN Publishing, Inc.
Jessica Lynn Curtis photograph copyright © 2012, Jason Campbell Photography
All Rights Reserved
Printed in China
First Printing

TRISTAN Publishing, Inc.
2355 Louisiana Avenue North
Golden Valley, MN 55427

To learn about all of our books with a message please visit
www.TRISTANpublishing.com

PAPA'S NEW HOME

by Jessica Lynn Curtis illustrated by Steve Harmon

TRISTAN PUBLISHING
Minneapolis

Some little girls are Daddy's girls. Others are Mommy's girls. Jessie was a Papa's girl. Each evening, before she could even talk, Jessie's Papa would carry her around the house they shared with her Nana, Mommy, and Daddy and teach her the words for everything they saw.

As soon as she could stand, Papa began measuring her against the garage and marking each little bit she grew. He taught Jessie to play catch, he let her help out in the garden, and she often heard him telling people, "Jessie is just the cat's pajamas!"

One morning, when she was three, Jessie awoke to find
Papa wasn't feeling well. He felt so awful, in fact, that Nana
took him to the hospital.

Jessie gave Papa a kiss goodbye, and hoped he would be
home soon. But as it turned out, Papa did not come home.
Instead, when Papa left the hospital, he moved someplace
very far away. He went to live in a place called Heaven.

When Papa went to Heaven, everyone was sad. Jessie said they should just go *visit* him, but Daddy explained that they couldn't visit Papa because he had *died* and become a spirit. He told Jessie she would see Papa again when she died and became a spirit in Heaven, too—but that for most people, that didn't happen until they were very old, with grandchildren and even *great* grandchildren of their own. Jessie didn't think she could wait that long.

Soon, Jessie missed Papa so much she couldn't bear it. She began having terrible dreams, and she cried all the time. Jessie didn't understand anything about Heaven or spirits— she just wanted her Papa!

One night, when Mommy tucked her into bed, she squeezed her extra tight and whispered, "I miss him, too, Jessie." When Mommy stood up, she wiped her eyes with the back of her hand. "Sweet dreams, jelly bean," she said. "I'll look in on you later and make sure you're not having a bad dream, okay?"

"Okay," said Jessie.

That was why, when Jessie felt someone sitting on her bed later, she figured it was just Mommy and didn't try to open her eyes.

"Jessie?" said a voice.

Jessie's eyes snapped open. It *was* her Papa! He had the same eyes, the same smile, the same bald head and round belly, but he looked different somehow. He was shiny and twinkly, like he was made of light!

"Papa!" Jessie cried out as she sat up and threw her arms around him. He squeezed her even tighter than Mommy had.

"I'm sorry you've been so sad, Jessie," said Papa.

"Why did you have to go to Heaven, Papa?" Jessie demanded. She let him go and crossed her arms. Jessie realized now she hadn't just been sad all these months. She was also *mad* at Papa for leaving her!

"Jessie," began Papa, "remember when you used to help me in the garden? Do you remember the time Papa's beautiful pink rosebush got sick?"

Jessie nodded.

"And no matter how hard I tried to save the rosebush," Papa continued, "it just got sicker and sicker, until finally its leaves turned brown and curled up. When that happened, it meant the rosebush had died."

"Like you did?" Jessie asked.

"Yes," Papa said gently, "just like I did. People are the same as plants. Animals, too. Our bodies aren't meant to live forever. They eventually get old or sick or hurt, and they stop working. But our *spirits*—our spirits *never* die."

"But what is a spirit?" asked Jessie.

"Well…" Papa said, "Do you notice how Papa looks a little different now?"

"Yes," Jessie said, "you're sparkly now!"

"Mmm hmm," said Papa. "Now I want you to look at *yourself* in the mirror."

Jessie went to her bedroom mirror.

"Do you see that light in your eyes?" Papa asked.

Jessie gasped. She had a light in her eyes that shined just like Papa!

"That light is your spirit shining through," Papa told her. "Your spirit is the very deepest part of you; it's who you are on the inside. And it's the part of you that will live forever."

"In Heaven?" Jessie asked.

"That's right," Papa said, "in Heaven."

"Will you take me there?" Jessie asked.

"Oh, Jessie… I'm really not supposed to. What if I just tell you about it?"

"Oh, please!" Jessie begged. "Please, please, *please* take me there!"

Papa sighed. He never *could* say no to Jessie! He scooped her into his arms and wrapped her in his bright, white light.

Jessie closed her eyes. When she opened them, she and Papa were in an enormous garden, surrounded by a million flowers, whose colors were a *zillion* times brighter than any Jessie had seen in her crayon box!

"Welcome to Heaven, Jessie! What would you like to see first?"

Jessie thought for a moment, then said, *"Everything!"*

Papa set Jessie down on the shimmery green grass. Beneath her bare feet, the grass felt softer than even her very softest pajamas.

Papa took Jessie's hand and began to lead her around the garden.

"This is my job in Heaven, Jessie," Papa told her. "I take care of all these flowers."

"There are *jobs* in Heaven?" Jessie asked.

"Mm hmm," Papa answered. "Your favorite thing to do on earth becomes your job in Heaven!"

He stopped walking and crouched down. "I want to show you something," he said, pointing to a plant that was the same height as Jessie.

She recognized it instantly—it was Papa's rosebush from the backyard! Jessie drew close to one beautiful pink rose. Its smell was even sweeter than it had been on earth, and there was something else—the rose was playing music!

"If you listen closely," Papa told Jessie, "everything in Heaven has its own song. When it all comes together, it's like nothing we could dream of on earth!"

"Let's hear *more* music, Papa!" she cried excitedly.

In the blink of an eye, Jessie and Papa were standing before a group of tall, magnificent spirits with golden halos and great, silver wings!

"This is the Choir of Angels," Papa explained.

The angels began to sing. The sound was so beautiful it made Jessie cry. She looked over at Papa and saw he had tears in his eyes, too.

Many songs later, Jessie and Papa continued their journey. They came upon a peaceful lake where people swam, sailed boats, and picnicked along the shore.

Everything Jessie saw—the water, the boats, and even the people—seemed to be made of light, just like Papa.

They passed through a glittering city, where all the buildings appeared to be made of colored crystals. When they passed a shiny purple building so tall Jessie was sure it had no end, Papa explained that this was the Library for All Time.

"It's so big," he said, "because it contains the answers to every question ever asked."

Papa laughed as Jessie's eyes widened.

"And now," Papa told Jessie, "I want to show you where I live!"

They both closed their eyes, and when they opened them, the ground was sandy and the air tasted like salt. They were in front of a big, white cottage beside a glimmering, blue-green ocean. As Jessie and Papa made their way toward the cottage, the front door opened and three dogs came bounding through. They ran down the front walk and began kissing Jessie.

"Jessie, these are Duchess, Penny, and Kiley. They were all your Mommy's dogs, and now they live with me in Heaven!"

As Jessie gasped delightedly, three smiling people came bustling through the door— a silver-haired man and woman, and a young man dressed like a soldier.

Papa beamed as he introduced them all. "This is my granddaughter, Jessie," he said. "Jessie, say hello to *my* Mommy and Daddy, your great grandparents; and this is my big brother, your Great Uncle Jerry."

Jessie smiled shyly as they all hugged and kissed her hello.

"See, Jessie?" said Papa. "Heaven is where everyone we love eventually goes—pets, too! It's where we're all together forever."

When Jessie imagined her whole family living together in this wonderful place, it filled her with such love and happiness she thought she might burst. She could feel herself beginning to glow, just like Papa.

"Why, Jessie, you must be starving!" her great grandmother said as she put an arm around Jessie and led her into the cottage. She sat Jessie down at a little table, where a cup of pink lemonade, a cream puff, three chocolate chip cookies, and a big piece of chocolate cake were waiting. As she ate, Jessie listened to stories about when Papa was small.

When she was finished, Papa wiped her mouth with a napkin, then picked her up and carried her around, showing her the pictures he had placed around the cottage. Some were of Jessie's Nana, and others were of Mommy and her two brothers.

"And this one," Papa said, pointing to a picture of two little girls, "is a picture of my granddaughters."

Jessie was confused. She could see that *she* was the older girl in the picture—but she didn't recognize the pretty baby beside her.

"That's your little sister, Jessie! Her name is Meagan. She'll be coming to meet you in eight months!"

Jessie's mouth fell open. Her very own baby sister! Suddenly, she wanted to go home. She knew she'd come back to Heaven someday, but right now, she had to get things ready for Baby Meagan!

"You're ready to go, Jessie?" Papa asked. Jessie nodded. She hugged and kissed everyone goodbye.

Jessie closed her eyes. When she opened them again, she and Papa were back in her bedroom. He tucked her into bed.

"Thank you for taking me to Heaven, Papa," Jessie said.

"I'm happy you got to see my new home, Jessie. Do you feel a little better now?"

"Yes," Jessie said, "but I'm going to miss you again when you go back."

"Jessie," Papa said, "I'll always be with you. Even when you can't see me, I'm with you, watching you from Heaven. You can talk to me, and I'll hear you. And if you let yourself be very still and quiet, and listen not just with your ears, but with your heart, you'll be able to hear me, too."

"I will," Jessie said. "I love you, Papa."

"I love you, too, Jessie. Sweet dreams, jelly bean." Papa kissed Jessie goodnight and he stayed with her until she fell asleep.

Jessie was still asleep when Mommy came into her room the next morning. Mommy woke her gently and asked, "Jessie, where did this flower come from?"

Jessie turned her head. Next to her on the pillow was Papa's pink rose from Heaven! She gasped happily, then told Mommy all about her visit.

That night, Jessie talked to Papa before she went to sleep. She knew he heard her, and when she listened with her heart, she heard him, too.